£29.50

Maths Outdoors

Carole Skinner

Acknowledgements

With thanks to those who trialled this book:

Lesley Addis, Blaenavon Hillside Nursery School, Torfaen

Jane Airey, Frith Manor Primary School, London

Amanda Aldridge, Gorse Hill Infant School, Swindon

Denise Bentham, Aston Clinton School, Aylesbury

Ann Dale, Paddox Primary School, Rugby

Donna Duffy, Fellbridge Primary School, West Sussex

Helen Elis Jones, University of Wales, Bangor, Gwynedd

Beverley Godfrey, South Wales Home-Educators Network, Pontyclun

Suzanne Hamilton, Education Effectiveness, Swansea

Margaret Latham, Grange over Sands CE Primary School, Cumbria

Nicola Laxton, St Paul's Infant School, Surrey

Trudy Lines, Bilbury School, Gloucestershire

Rachel Mansley, Cottam Primary School, Preston

Sol Mattu, Townhill Community School, Swansea

Lindsay Mihailovic, St Edmund's Nursery School, Bradford

Sarah Phelps, Clydach Infant School, Swansea

Jane Prothero, Woodlands Primary, Leeds

Sheila Stringer, St Hilary's School, Surrey

Louise Stubbs, Roberttown Junior and Infant School, West Yorkshire

Ruth Trundley, Devon Curriculum Services, Exeter

Suzanne Turner, Golborne St Thomas CE J&I School, Cheshire

Sandra Whitaker, Gayhurst School, Bucks

Thanks also to Jean Miller, Nicola Hall, and The BEAM Development Group

Special thanks to Jan White, Senior Early Years Development Officer, Learning through Landscapes www.ltl.org.uk. Learning through Landscapes is the national school grounds charity that works with schools and early years settings to support them in the use and development of their outdoor provision.

Published by BEAM Education
Maze Workshops
72a Southgate Road
London N1 3JT
Telephone 020 7684 3323
Fax 020 7684 3334
Email info@beam.co.uk
www.beam.co.uk
© Beam Education 2005
ISBN 978 1 9031 4236 3
British Library Cataloguing-in-Publication Data
Data available
Edited by Raewyn Glynn
Designed by Malena Wilson-Max
Illustrations by Ken Wilson-Max
Photographs by Len Cross

Thanks to College Gardens Nursery School and Maxilla Nursery School

Printed in England by Cromwell Press Ltd

Reprinted in 2007.

Young children need to experience mathematical concepts through their bodies in practical experiences that make sense to them. When children have repeated experiences involving their whole bodies and with high levels of engagement, deep-level learning takes place through changes in the structure of the brain: the child really understands and new thinking abilities grow.

The outdoor environment can provide engaging and meaningful experiences for young children, allowing them to learn in ways that suit them best. This wonderful environment offers endless contexts that intrigue and involve children and they are able to draw on their everyday playful explorations to investigate and use mathematical thinking, from the tiny to the grand scale. What better way to learn about volume, weight and distance than by filling a wheelbarrow with soil or gravel and transporting it across the outdoor space?

Taking learning outdoors to where young children are stimulated and learn best is one of the most effective things we can do to make maths enjoyable, interesting and easy to understand. Creating a mathematical environment outside, making the most of practical situations and creative problem solving, will result in young learners who are confident with the number system and who will comfortably apply mathematical ideas to new situations. Young children often reveal high levels of understanding and competency when playing with maths outside, so use these opportunities to observe and assess, too.

Maths Outdoors gives an excellent overview for this area of learning and provides practitioners with many accessible and realistic starting points for taking maths outside with success. I hope it will give you the confidence to be enthusiastic and inventive in using your own outdoor space to great effect.

Jan White

Senior Development Officer for Early Years,
Learning through Landscapes

Contents

Chapter 1

Creating an outdoor maths environment

Maths and outdoor play

Outdoor play is a powerful learning medium for children. When playing outdoors, children have the opportunity to try out new ideas and mathematical skills such as counting and measuring, as well as developing their imagination and creativity on a large scale. The outdoor environment offers children as much opportunity for active learning as the best-planned indoor area.

To be successful, maths learning needs to involve children in doing, thinking and playing. It should be interactive, ensuring that children are directors of the action as well as enthusiastic participants and that they have time to reflect on what happens. It is crucial that what children are engaged in is meaningful to them, and creative in the human sense, so that they come to understand maths through movement, through making images, through exploring using all their senses and through play.

Setting up your outdoor environment

A high-quality maths environment outdoors can often take time to set up. This is especially true if you involve the children in the setting up — but both you and the children will learn a lot in the process. Take their suggestions on identifying different zones or areas in your

"This week, let's have a voting booth where we can decide what colour to paint the bus."

outdoor space. Together, you can build temporary structures with poles and trellises to differentiate your areas.

Suggested zones or areas may include a sand area, a water area, a gardening and wildlife area, a sensory area, a writing area, a theatre and storytelling area, a music area, and a quiet area

Do not be discouraged if your outdoor area is mostly asphalt playground. Plant it up using large pots, tree-trunks and grow-bags as well as low-level hanging baskets.

"Can you find your way out of the sand area using Louise's map?"

Encourage the children to draw their own maps of the different zones in the outdoor area where things can be found as well as notices that say what to look for. Laminate signs and posters for use outdoors.

Dismantling and rebuilding can also contribute to children's learning in design and technology. Just as the children are involved in helping put together an outdoor area that works for them, they also need to be part of the taking down, changing or putting away. When children have helped to put together role-play areas, these areas are more effective if children give permission for changes to be made.

Suggested resources

Put together learning resources that are versatile, such as plastic crates, guttering, washing lines and small carpet squares. Permanent fixtures often have just one use. It is more effective to encourage children to control, change and modify their environment. It's up to us to use resources that empower children and that they identify with. That way, they will get maximum learning from their outdoor area.

Invest in some hanging shoe-tidies as containers for resources and suspend them from a washing line. Hang different peg baskets from the line filled with sorting materials. Use them as holders of collections. For more ideas, choose from the list of general resources on page 9 or the list of maths resources on page 80.

Outdoor resource suggestions

General

- A-frame ladders
- Canopies for shade/shelter
- Climbing frame
- Guttering
- Imitation railway sleepers
- Large blankets, plastic sheets, bubble-wrap, tarpaulins, silver 'emergency' space blankets...
- Outside tap
- Pond liner
- Sandpit with buckets, spades, wheelbarrows...
- Shallow builder's tray
- Large water tray with objects for floating and sinking such as corks...
- Wheeled vehicles with bikes, go-carts, trolleys, pushchairs
- Wooden logs for seats/rolling
- Tin bath
- Tree trunk for balancing

Weather and protective resources

- Umbrellas (for rain and shade)
- Waterproof clothing
- Wellies
- Woollen gloves
- Plastic gloves
- Gardening gloves
- Clothes horse and table cloth
- Trellis as windbreak
- Curtains

Time

- One-minute sand timers
- Stopwatches

- Sundial
- Tocker timers

For quiet area

- Different-shaped cushions
- Stories with number and outdoor themes (laminated and spiral-bound for outdoors)
- Beanbags for sitting

Patterns

- Decorating brushes and bowls
- Foam decorating rollers
- Hand-held lens (magnifying glass)
- Luminous paint
- Pieces of bark
- Rakes for sand
- Shells and pebbles
- Small hand brooms and yard brooms/brushes
- Twigs
- Wax crayons and paper to make wax rubbings

Natural world maths

- Bird trays/table
- Bug boxes
- Compost/grow-bags
- Gardening tools (spades, rakes, hoes, trowels...)
- Plant pots
- Plant sprayers
- Plastic fish tank
- Plastic spoons (for carrying mini-beasts)
- Seed trays
- Seeds, including grass seed

- Telescopes
- Torches
- Watering cans
- Flexible hoses

Musical maths

- Dustbin lids
- Tin mugs and plates and cans
- Wind chimes made from old cutlery, tins and jar lids
- Wooden spoons (as beaters)

ICT

- Calculators
- Cash registers
- Digital microscope
- Laptop computers (battery-powered)
- Mobile phones
- Programmable toys
- Tape recorder and headphones (battery powered)
- Video and digital camera
- Walkie-talkies

Small equipment

- Balloon pumps and balloons
- Bubble mix and bubble blowers
- Mirrors
- Reflective materials such as foil
- Windmills and kites
- Parachute
- Pulleys
- Washing line and pegs
- Assorted plastic mixing bowls
- Shopping baskets
- Baking tray
- Ribbons for weaving

Outdoor area plan

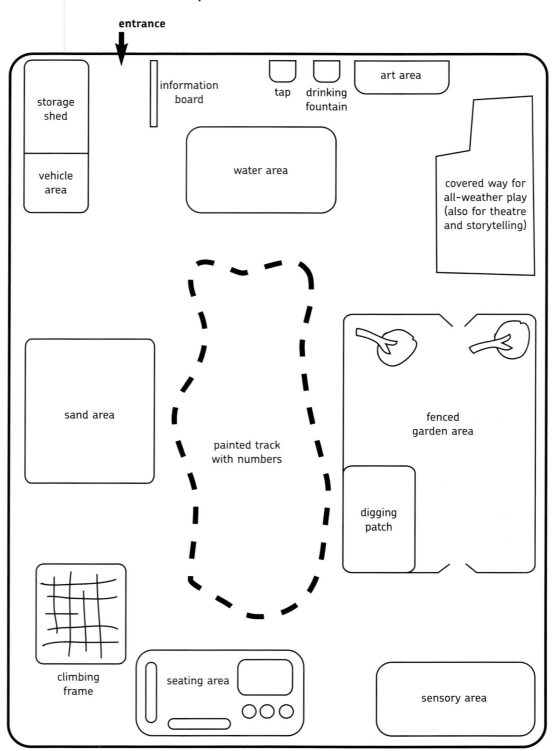

Taking on the weather

The unique learning opportunities that the outdoor area provides should not be defeated by the weather. Put together a weather resource box that contains small umbrellas, plastic hooded ponchos and waterproofs, as well as a supply of wellington boots. Use large golf umbrellas as shelter from the rain (and use as sunshades in the summer). Invest in plastic gazebos with sides that provide protection from rain and can also double up as role-play areas. Use suspended shower curtains and roller blinds to provide cover over sand and water trays.

Use a blanket with a waterproof backing or a groundsheet with a blanket on top so that the children can sit on the ground to use building materials and small world characters. Peg down pieces of bubble wrap on the grass to provide a seating area if the ground is damp. Try using bubble wrap over a tent frame or stapled to a clotheshorse to provide a light, protected working area.

Cold weather will require a ready supply of woolly hats, scarves and gloves, as well as some protection from the wind. Ideal activities for cold weather will include lots of moving about, for example zigzagging between lines of plastic cones or scootering round a numbered obstacle course in the right order.

On sunny days, shade is a consideration. Using large umbrellas positioned in places where children will be working for a substantial amount of time is a quick and easy solution. Tie muslin sheets at the corners using string and suspend over track or games areas. Erect a large cotton triangular sail on top of the climbing frame to provide shade for climbers (the shadow shapes this makes can also be a talking point). Investing in awnings over windows will protect the children indoors and provide shade for those working outdoors.

Developing your outdoor learning areas

The theatre and storytelling area

If you can squeeze in a space — even the smallest is better than none — try to construct a stage area where children can perform, listen and dance to number rhymes and songs. The area will need to be resourced with appealing props so that children will respond when you invite them to retell a story. Once you have a storytelling area, you will find that everybody will want to re-enact stories such as *Where's the Bear?* and *We're Going on a Bear Hunt*. It just seems that stories that are located outdoors need to be brought outdoors to get the horizon and the atmosphere right. Performing them outdoors also helps the sequencing that goes on. Stories with a lot of repetition, such as *Look Out! It's the Wolf*, are especially effective. Stage an outdoor concert event and provide blankets and umbrellas for the audience. Use musical instruments or a tambourine to alert the children that the production is about to begin.

The sand area

When creating a sand area, capitalize on the special nature of the outdoors — the freedom it gives to make a mess, deal with a larger scale expanse of sand or dig deeper into the sand. Removing socks and shoes and wriggling toes in the sand leads inevitably to making footprints and then lines of footprints, which will need to be counted, and their shapes compared. Try to be creative about positioning the sand area — many garden edgings such as jointed log rolls will restrict the sand to one place if that is an issue, or you can use a deep preformed garden pond. Putting a wooden plank across a ready-built sand pit will give children a different perspective on their sand constructions and also develop their balancing skills.

As well as changing the shape and size of the sand area, you could replace the sand with dried crushed leaves, sawdust or rice to extend the children's experiences.

Encourage the children to observe closely the tools and equipment they are using. For example, talk about why some containers fit inside others and some do not, how sand slithers down the side of a funnel and forms a cone shape, and whether the size of hole means the bucket empties faster. A wide range of equipment will encourage children's experimentation and observation in activities such as finding out how many different shapes they can make with damp sand.

Put natural materials such as twigs, shells and small stones into the sand container and discuss anything children observe. Include magnifying glasses and binoculars so that children can experiment with looking at things smaller and larger.

"Do you think you'll find a twig longer than this one in the sand?"

The water area

Wherever you position your water area, make sure that you are close to a tap to give children access to running water and enable them to play with hoses. You can establish water areas using construction bricks and pond liners that are different shapes and sizes and that need only last for a week. These can provide topics for discussion.

Fill a large container with water and add some balloons (make sure they are anchored to a stone or brick). Or shallow-fill a container with water, add some large porridge oats and provide whisks. Try cooked long spaghetti and tongs, spaghetti spoons and dinner forks.

Instead of water, some days fill a large container with strips or pieces of multi-coloured cellophane or other transparent material and pretend play with water.

In winter, fill a plastic paddling pool with water. Use different-sized containers as boats. Attach different-shaped sails made from materials such as paper, foil, tissue and polythene, and explore ways of attaching the sails. Number the boats. Discuss different ways of making the boats sail further or faster, such as using hand-held battery fans or blowing through straws.

Develop children's imaginative play by borrowing and setting up for a few weeks a full-sized canoe, a small dinghy with a sail or a real rowing boat with oars. Provide waterproofs and life jackets.

The garden area

In a small area, put down plastic sheeting and surround it with logs. Cover the sheeting with bark and arrange one or two large shrubs in pots. The children now have a different type of floor covering to comment on. Use hanging baskets at child height and involve children in planting and watering. Together, draw up a rota for basket-maintenance tasks such as watering and deadheading the plants.

"How many handfuls of bark do you think it will take to fill your bucket? Close your eyes and describe what the bark feels like."

Set up a potting table resourced with compost, bulbs, small bedding plants and plastic pots. Pot up all the plants and decide how many pots will be needed. Decide how far up the pot the compost should come, and how deep to plant the bulbs or plants. Water the pots.

Design and make a mini-beast nature reserve in your wildlife area. Encourage earwigs by resting flowers pots on their sides and filling with straw. Let woodlice live in a pile of logs and roof tiles. Find snails underneath large damp stones. Keep records and charts of what mini-beasts you see in the nature reserve. Draw a map of where each species can be seen. Make a tape recording of what to look for and how to care for the mini-beasts in your area. Provide soft paintbrushes to move mini-beasts instead of handling them.

Music-making

Children can use maths as they explore making music outdoors. This is a great opportunity to make extra-loud sounds that might be overwhelming indoors. Make a music line by numbering metal dustbin lids, saucepans, tin plates and mugs and tying them to a washing line. Provide wooden spoons as sound-makers.

To the spokes of an open umbrella, tie a collection of small percussion objects such as spoons, forks, tin cans and jam jar lids. Give the children an assortment of beaters to use. Discuss how many times they 'beat' each object and look for a pattern in the music. Make music in the rain under a large umbrella — try to make the sounds of the raindrops.

The sensory area

Set up large pots with plants that are interesting to touch and smell, including herbs such as rosemary, lavender and sage. Include plants where the leaves need to be handled to release their scent, as well as scented flowers such as honeysuckle and wallflowers

Install a range of wind chimes made by the children as well as soft drums and rain shakers. Put out bowls containing a variety of small smooth pebbles and shells to handle, count and make patterns with.

Set up a reflection site and involve the children in noticing how things look when they are seen through mirrors. Draw attention to the site by suspending a shiny silver 7 ft x 5 ft (210 cm x 150 cm) 'emergency space blanket' as a backdrop and using it for large-scale reflections. These blankets are very reasonable to buy. Use child-sized space blankets to play wrapping up games. Wrap each other up to keep warm and wrap soft toys in shiny material. Talk about size as the children are busy wrapping. Use a torch to reflect shadows onto foil paper. Use a large mirror to make an outdoor vista. Or use distorting mirrors. Have children hold a mirror up on a level with their eyes and observe what's happening behind them. Ask them to describe what they can see.

Your role in the outdoor learning environment

The role of the adult is to make sure the outdoor environment is visually rich and exciting and then to engage children's curiosity and challenge their understanding. In order to ensure children get the most benefit from the outdoor learning area, you will need to:

- give children a synopsis of each activity, so that they have an idea of the big picture

The adult's role:

* encourage
* join in
* listen
* talk
* discuss
* share
* identify
* assess
* observe
* initiate
* extend
* challenge
* question

"Look, Alex and Su Lin are using the metre sticks. They have discovered a way of measuring the fence. Why don't you ask them to show you?"

Our Outdoors Scrapbook

- use mathematical language with the children and encourage them to use it too by making questioning statements such as, "I wonder if you've got more than me..."

- make sure that you use the key words you have identified in your planning, and that the children use them in discussion

- value children's ideas and allow them to explain what they think before you intervene

- give children time to review and reflect upon what has happened as the activity finishes. You can do this as you are helping children to tidy up. "I noticed you were working with the blocks. Do you think there is another way we could sort them?"

Maintain interest in the outdoor area by issuing a weekly 'Outside News' bulletin. Identify what is new each week, include photos of children working outdoors and identify the learning that is going on. Use captions such as "Here is Maya putting the numbers in order". Invite adults and other helpers to be involved.

Encourage children to develop their mathematical ideas and skills by exploring and investigating as they play. You can do this by using mathematical words in your discussions. Make observations such as "I wonder if there are any stones heavier than this one..." Give directions on how to find a hidden object by saying, "Teddy is hiding next to something taller than you." Support younger children by describing what they are doing as they play.

There are various ways we can help children to understand mathematical ideas, including providing children with opportunities to talk and think about what they have done and make connections between experiences, and asking questions that extend children's previous answers, such as: "What else can you think of?" and "How can we check what we found out?"

Mathematical recording

Children will want to record their experiences of counting and measuring, and they will need to make those recordings in a variety of ways. Talking about and discussing what happened is a very important first and major way of recording for everybody. At other times, photographs, tape recordings, constructions, plans and diagrams will be a more appropriate form of recording. Writing and drawing can also be efficient ways of recording, or use computers and calculators. You can support children's reflections on the experiences and their recording by encouraging discussion and talk and giving easy access to recording resources. By providing materials such as paper, pens and clipboards in all areas of interest, children will be able to also represent their experiences and observations immediately as another way of making a permanent record to discuss later.

Station easels in various places with a chalkboard, or attach paper and large felt-tip pens to make spontaneous mark-making more likely. Resource games areas with small chalkboards and clipboards for recording scores. Make sure there is a laminated number line in sight. Hook up plant or vegetable hanging baskets to store wooden numerals in the games zone, so that children can pick up the numeral that represents their score.

If it's possible, paint a hard surface area on the wall that the children can write on. Provide a lot of different places that give children the opportunity to draw, write and record maths.

Extending the potential of outdoor learning areas

Obstacle coursing: Set up a mini obstacle course using wooden ramps and blocks in the construction zone and invite children to roll balls round the course. Children can also design and build their own course.

Viewing: Construct a viewing platform using staging blocks or secure a balancing plank between two bars of the climbing frame. Equip with binoculars and charge 10p admittance to look at the view and 10p to take photographs. Arrange artefacts to make a more interesting view, if necessary.

Collecting: Make a collection of leaves and see how many different browns, reds, yellows and greens you can find. Put them in order from darkest to lightest. Provide colour charts for colour matching, then mix the colours with paints.

Texturing: Collect several objects with different textures and say ways to describe them. Compare similarities and differences between objects. Wrap objects in foil paper and feel them. Say what they are. Carefully remove the foil so that you can still see the imprint of the object. Alternatively, leave out sheets of foil and textured objects for children to wrap and smooth over to show texture.

Cementing: Use sand and cement together to make landscapes on a builder's tray. Leave to dry, then spatter paint using a toothbrush. Discuss the shapes on the landscape and the mountains and valleys.

Picnicking: Pack up some food and drink in a basket. Write some menus and take a camera, then journey to the farthest corner of your grounds and have a picnic.

Treasuring: Make up small treasure baskets containing natural objects such as conkers, fir cones and smooth pebbles for children to use in play. Or supply plastic film containers for the children to fill with 'jewels' and bury in the sand tray. Draw a map to show where the treasure is buried.

Tossing: Lay a parachute or tablecloth on the ground and cover with dry leaves. Hold the edges of the sheet and toss the leaves into the air. Try to make sure that all the leaves are caught again in the parachute.

Bottling: Arrange a supply of small plastic water bottles and a

"How can we find out how many leaves we've collected?"

hosepipe along with bottle carriers, cardboard wine carriers (from supermarkets), milk crates or wine racks. Encourage children to organise a bottled-water delivery service and a recycling store of empty bottles.

Parking: Create a vehicle area. Mark out numbered parking bays for bikes and cars. Invent a booking system for the vehicles; make sure that there are sufficient number labels and writing materials.

Car washing: Convert part of the vehicle area to a car wash. Resource with buckets, soapy water, sponges, water cans and hoses. Decide on the price list. Put together a 'workers' rota' of days and times.

Reflecting: Cut up and hang foil strips, curls and spirals along with CDs. Fill a shallow pond liner with water to make a puddle and look at each other's reflection. Make a pretend puddle with silver foil for the small world characters.

ICT: Raising awareness of everyday technology

Everyday technology will play an important part in children's lives. Therefore, planning specific activities that involve using technology will support children's skill development and understanding. You will find it useful to do an audit of the ICT resources that are specifically for use in your outdoor environment. Many early years teachers find that their ICT resources are only occasionally being used outdoors, mostly when taken there by the children. Play and learning can be enriched when the resources are readily available outdoors already and are part of planned activities.

ICT resource suggestions

Technology resource	Activities	Learning
Programmable toys such as Roamer, Pixie, Bee Bot Robots	• Inputting instructions • Attaching pens to draw the route toys take	• Sequencing • Using positional language
Mobile phones	• Giving and taking messages • Organising an orderline or answering service	• Saying numbers • Speaking and listening
Walkie talkie	• Relaying information • Giving directions • Repeating instructions	• Using everyday words to describe a route
Calculator	• Putting in numbers • Using as a digital counter to record the number of children outdoors or cars in the car park	• Recognising numerals • Clearing memory • Keeping running totals
Video and digital cameras	• Filming an activity or drama • Taking photographs on a journey or trail	• Reflecting • Organising and sequencing
Battery-powered laptop computer	• Gathering, sorting and entering information on found items	• Data handling • Pressing keys
Battery-powered tape recorder and headphones	• Recording sounds, traffic, birds, children • Following headphone instructions on a trail or guided tour of area	• Data handling and sound recognition • Using positional language
Digital microscope	• Closely examining mini-beasts, leaves, flower-heads and found items	• Questioning, sorting and counting
Cash registers with 'card swipe'	• Modelling entering numbers • Using money	• Talking about numbers and recognising coins

Chapter 2

The early learning goals

Supporting and assessing mathematical development

In this section you will find activities and experiences to support children working at different levels of Foundation Stage learning. While there are specific activities for assessment purposes, give observational insights into children's mathematical understanding. We also offer ideas for sustaining and extending children's thinking and we relate them to individual learning intentions. While there are aspects of the *Curriculum guidance for the foundation stage* that interlink — and we know that children learn in a cross-curricular way — we have centred the learning on the early learning goals for mathematical development to help you clearly identify children's progress.

For planning and assessment purposes, early learning goals are divided into three aspects reflecting mathematical learning and key skills:

Learning about number
The first aspect of mathematical development focuses on numbers as labels and for counting. This involves working towards being able to say the number names in order, match the number to objects counted and know that you say one number for each object you count, as well as knowing that the last number you say is the number of objects in the collection.

Learning about addition and subtraction

The second aspect of mathematical development focuses on calculating in a practical context. This involves comparing numbers of objects, combining numbers of objects and using the related vocabulary such as 'more' and 'less', and being able to find one more and one less practically.

Learning shape, space and measure

The third aspect of mathematical development relates to shape, space and measures. The emphasis is always on children experiencing the properties of shape and space in practical contexts such as construction play and pattern work. The understanding of measurement will develop from activities that are based on direct comparison of sizes and quantities as well as on activities that involve filling, emptying and constructing.

Developing a mathematical vocabulary

A further important aspect of mathematical learning and understanding is becoming familiar with and using mathematical vocabulary. Children's mathematical vocabulary is enhanced when adults who are working alongside them:

- repeat key words in context during play activities

- encourage children to use new words through questioning

- ask children to describe what they see, hear or think

We recognise that all children learn more maths through interaction with adults and the exploration of the world around them. We also know that children learn more when they are allowed to make decisions, choices and mistakes. Children benefit enormously from the support of a knowledgeable adult and from being respected as autonomous and competent learners.

When we are generating a community of learners, everyone needs time and space in which to articulate his or her thinking. Inviting children to explain how they worked something out will provide an opportunity for some children to say what they are thinking. Although listening to other children's explanations is valuable, it is no substitute for explaining yourself. When children work together in pairs they can say what they are thinking, listen to one another and support each other's learning in a safe situation.

Working with number outdoors

Learning intentions

* ✳ Recognise the numerals 1–9 and beyond
* ✳ Use the number names appropriately
* ✳ Begin to write the numerals 1–9
* ✳ Count a variety of objects

Counting (a large group activity)
Make an interactive dinosaur counting-line by attaching some numbered counting bags in order to a fence and asking the children to put the appropriate number of dinosaurs in each bag. You can extend the activity by changing the objects in the bag to shells or teddies or by arranging the bags in a random order.

One by one (a pairs activity)
Put small characters in the water tray and ask the children to use a tea strainer to scoop them up. Ask the children to count how many they collected in their scoop. Extend the activity by challenging children to use tongs to pick up one character at a time until they have collected five. Alternatively, use the tongs to 'rescue' five characters onto a boat that is floating on the water tray.

Recognising numerals *(a pairs activity)*
Bury wooden or plastic numerals in a bag of compost. Invite children
to find a particular number, using plastic spades to dig for the
numerals. The children could then bury the numerals themselves or
look for a missing number suggested by one of the children.

Number partners *(a large group activity)*
Distribute at least two of every numeral and ask the children to find a
partner who is holding the same numeral as themselves.

Reading numerals *(a small group activity)*
Make a picture gallery of numbers made from twigs, arranged stones
and other found materials. Extend the activity by putting the numbers
in order. Ask the children to make a number more than 5, or between
3 and 6.

Spaghetti numbers *(a small group activity)*
Using a packet of long pasta such as spaghetti, dip each strip into a
bowl of water and then model the strips into numbers.

Recognising numerals (a small group activity)
Make a number tree with a large branch set into a
bucket of earth and ask the children to hang
different numerals on the branches. Change the
numbers frequently to maintain a talking point.
One week have all the same number, at other times have
random numbers or choose two numbers such as 3 and 5.
Extend the activity by attaching paper clips to wooden or
plastic numerals, dangling magnets from the tree and challenging
the children to put the numbers onto the magnets in order.

Paint by numbers (a pairs activity)
Provide an assortment of empty washing-up bottles filled with water
and encourage the children to 'write' a number on the ground or wall
using the bottles. You can extend the activity by providing large sheets
of paper and filling the bottles with paint or, on another day, by using
small spray bottles filled with water and 'writing' the numbers in a
sand tray or tray of coloured gravel.

Number seeds (a small group activity)
Put out a large bowl of bird seed. Ask the children to write a number
on the ground in bird seed using a paper cone that has a small hole
cut across the end. Extend the learning by asking the children to
chalk out the number first and then sprinkle it with seed. You could
also make the numbers using grass seed on the lawn area or cress
seed on pieces of damp muslin.

Ordering numbers (a pairs activity)
Suspend five numbered hoops in order on a washing line, making
sure the hoops are low enough to climb through. Ask the children to
climb through the hoops in number order. Extend the activity by
putting the hoops in a random order, but asking the children to climb
through in the right order. Alternatively, number the hoops 2 to 6 or
use the numbers 5, 6, 7, 8 and 9.

A large group
assessment activity

Learning assessment

❋ Can the children
  continue the count
  from a given number?

❋ Can they say the
  number after any
  number up to 9
  or 10 or 12?

Circle rounds

You will need

❋ a collection of soft toys or beanbags

❋ a washing-up bowl

What to do

1. Select a number between, say, 3 and 7. Ask the children to start counting round the circle from that number until they get to the number 12. Whoever says 10 in the count has to collect a beanbag from the centre.

2. Play a couple of rounds of 'whoever says 10' and then describe a number. For example, say, "Whoever says one more than 9." Then choose another range such as "Start counting from 2 to 12".

A large group
assessment activity

Learning assessment

❋ Can the children count
  out objects from a
  larger group?

❋ Can they recognise
  numerals up to 10?

Counting everything

You will need

❋ a collection of bears, dinosaurs, elephants and other counting materials (at least fifteen of each type)

❋ small containers for sorting

❋ two packs of 1–10 cards, shuffled

❋ a small plastic bucket to be the 'counted' bucket

What to do

1. Ask the children to sort everything into separate containers, for example the bears into one dish, the elephants into another and so on.

2. Put a small bucket in the centre of the group.

3. Invite a child to take the top card from the pack and put that many objects from one of the sorted collections into the bucket.

4. Keep taking turns until all the materials are in the counted bucket.

Matchmaking

You will need

※ a pack of giant 0–10 number cards

※ packs of 0–10 number cards

What to do

1. Give each child a variety of number cards from the packs.

2. Show the children one of the giant number cards. If they are holding a card that added to the giant card makes 10, they shout, "Match."

Simplification

Shout "Match" if the two numbers are the same. Or use number cards 0–5 and find pairs to make 5.

Learning assessment

※ Can the children recognise numerals up to 5?

※ Can they recognise numerals up to 10?

Addition and subtraction outdoors

Adding and subtracting activities for young children need to be rooted in real situations. Look for and invent situations that mean together you can use the language of addition and subtraction.

Learning intentions

※ Use the language of addition and subtraction.

※ Find one more and one less than a number from 1 to 10.

※ Begin to relate addition to combining two groups of objects and subtraction to taking away.

Shape and space outdoors

> ### Learning intentions
>
> ❋ Use language to describe the shape and size of solids and flat shapes and begin to name them.
>
> ❋ Talk about, recognise and recreate simple patterns.
>
> ❋ Use everyday words to describe position.

Salt spray (small group activity)

Fill small plastic squeezy bottles with cooking salt and draw straight and curved lines or use to draw patterns. Extend the learning by suspending the container upside down on string and letting it swing.

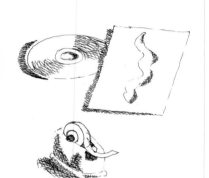

Silhouettes (small group activity)

Arrange some small flattish objects or shapes on paper. Ask children to choose an object, spray paint over it and remove to show the silhouette.

Extend the learning by making a display of silhouettes and asking children to guess which shape made each silhouette.

Rolling balls (large group activity)

Paint large sheets of paper on the ground using rollers. Dip rubber balls into water and roll across the paper. Extend the learning by dipping balls in different paint colours and rolling them across the paper. Also try using balls attached to elastic to bounce on the paper.

Rolling balls (small group activity)

Put circles of paper on large tin trays. Dip small balls into paint and roll across the tray. Extend the learning by using small lids and rolling paint dipped marbles.

Flags *(small group activity)*

Make flag strings by using 2D flat shapes as templates and drawing round the edges onto pieces of fabric to make flags. Staple the different-shaped flags to a thin strip of material. Suspend the flag strings between two posts or trees.

Extend the learning by stapling flags onto straws or sticks and use in the sand tray to show where the same shapes are buried.

Chalk painting *(small group activity)*

Put some small pieces of chalk (used ones are fine) into a plastic bag and, using pastry rolling pins or small cylinders, roll the chalks until they are crushed and mostly powdered. Tip the powder into a small container and add enough water to make a runny paint. Use the mixture to paint patterns and shapes on the ground or wall. When the session is finished, it is almost as much fun using a watering can or hose to remove the paintings.

Assessing shape

A small group assessment activity

You will need

* two collections of similar solid and flat shapes. Each collection should contain two different types of triangles, different-sized circles, squares and rectangles as well as a cube, a cylinder and another 3D shape. For younger children, you may wish to restrict the shape collection to two or three shapes.

What to do

Hide every shape from one of the collections within a contained area such as the garden or climbing area. Give the children a shape each and ask them to look for another shape the same. Discuss the names of the shapes together.

Learning assessment

* Can the children use mathematical language to describe solid and flat shapes?
* Can they use developing mathematical ideas about shape and space to solve problems?

Measures outdoors

Learning intentions

※ Use language such as 'more' or 'less', 'longer' or 'shorter', 'heavier' or 'lighter' to compare length, mass or capacity.

Gunge (small group activity)

Before the session dissolve soap flakes (1 cup of soap flakes into 2 litres of warm water) in a large bowl. Add a few drops of food colouring and whisk with a hand-held or electric mixer until the mixture looks like mousse. Provide small containers and different-sized spoons for the children to fill.

Extend the learning by putting the mousse into icing bags and syringes for the children to pipe round the edges of containers.

A pairs assessment activity

Learning assessment

※ Can the children use developing mathematical ideas about comparing quantities to solve mathematical problems?

What size is it?

You will need

✳ two small cups or beakers differing slightly in size

✳ dry sand or rice

✳ plastic cubes

✳ a 1-litre container

What to do

Ask the children to find out which cup holds the most. Encourage them to talk about the method they are using to solve the problem. Ask questions such as "What are you trying to find out?" or "Is there another way you could try?"

Ten further activities for exploring measures

Learning	Group size	Activity
Using capacity language	Pairs	Put a dinosaur in a box inside a box.
Using capacity language	Small group	Fill a range of small boxes with collections of things.
Using the language of length	Small group	Choose a ribbon from a collection and then find a longer one.
Using the language of length	Pairs	Use large plastic bricks to make a line across the construction area.
Using the language of length	Large group	Hold hands and make a line across the outdoor area.
Using the language of time	Large group	Write a weekly name timetable for using wheeled toys.
Using the language of time	Large group	Put together a 'before and after' exhibition, using photos, models and paintings.
Using the language of weight	Pairs	Choose an object and together search for something heavier.
Using the language of weight	Small group	Fill up two shopping baskets and say which one is heaviest.
Using the language of height	Pairs	Together, build the tallest tower using three boxes.

Chapter 3

Outdoor maths games

Why play games?

Games are a wonderful way for children to learn maths and enjoy themselves at the same time. Playing of games is also a major factor in supporting and reinforcing children's understanding of numbers, as well as a useful way of encouraging speaking and listening and other communication skills. For children, some of the best things about playing games, especially outdoors, are that you can make a lot of noise, talk a lot,

jump about, skip, hop, roll balls, aim beanbags and puzzle over things with your friends. Young children enjoy playing games and solving problems and that's a good way to start to learn maths.

Fun and games

Having fun together is an important part of children playing games. However, it is always better to invite children to join in with a game instead of stating that now they are going to play such and such a game. One of the advantages of invented games over bought or published games is that by using different equipment the game will seem different to the children, yet still have the familiarity of known procedures. Even varying the way of moving along a number track,

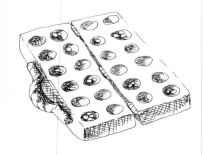

hopping instead of jumping, walking backwards instead of forwards will make the game seem a new game. Many traditional board games which develop mathematical skills can be recreated outdoors by scaling up the board layouts and modelling large counters where needed. Traditional games such as 'Snakes and Ladders' and 'Mancala' will have a different feel when played on a large scale outdoors, but even just playing them the same size is a valuable experience.

Establish and continue a games-playing ethos with large space games such as 'What's the time, Mr Wolf?' and 'Grandmother's footsteps'. These games are ideal for young children outdoors, helping them to get their bearings and come to terms with operating in a large area. As well as games that generate scoring systems, play games that use tallying, such as finding out how many beanbags in a crate. Or make a game of jumping along a line or track to place a dice.

While outdoors, make sure there is spontaneous singing that involves action rhymes and number rhymes. There are many rhymes and stories that involve mathematical ideas and provide a relaxed and social way of learning about numbers and counting. Many rhymes have traditional games associated with them, for example, 'Ring-a-Ring o' Roses', 'Oranges and Lemons' and 'Here We Go 'round the Mulberry Bush'. All of these and many others give children the opportunity to link actions with words as well as quite often containing an element of sequencing. And of course you can adapt the words or the actions to fit the circumstances. The children will be learning informal adding and subtracting and the order of the number names, forwards and backwards. Ask questions such as "Would it work if we used different numbers?"

"Do you think there will still be eight counters if I count them in a different order?"

In order to support younger children or inexperienced game players, you will need to keep the group playing the game small. This will mean they have more participation and each player will have more chances to learn and practise skills. Generally, adapting a game to make it smaller (for instance, fewer children playing), slower (for instance, only one child throwing a beanbag at any one time) or easier (for instance, only using numbers up to 3) will mean it is more accessible for younger children. In this way, you make the game suit the player rather than the other way round.

Games and counting

In order to get the most from playing games, at the end of the play encourage the children to recount any collections of objects they may have by starting the count from a different object.

Children really do need to use the counting sequence in as many different contexts as possible to be confident with the number system. You could also use the opportunity to develop their estimation skills by asking them to predict before they count their collections.

And a good games rule to have when using a dice is "We always say the number that we roll". This helps children who are just beginning to read numerals or recognise spot patterns as well as supporting children for whom English is an additional language.

Keeping score

We know that children learn best about recording numbers when they are doing so in practical situations. When playing games, children are likely to understand the purpose of the recording. Provide plenty of equipment for mark-making, such as chalkboards and easels, and encourage children to keep scores and record game results. Scores do not have to be kept in a competitive way, but rather as data collection, or as a comparison of what happened. The board could on some occasions be labelled 'These are the dice numbers we rolled'.

The games in this section all have suggested adaptations for younger children, as well as extensions for older or more experienced children. In addition, we have identified the main learning opportunities — although of course other maths learning is likely to occur as well. We also suggest how the game can be played the following day to make it seem a new game to the children.

Hoopla

You will need

❋ six hoops

❋ six pieces of card numbered 1–6

❋ a large 1–6 dice

❋ a collection of small soft toys

❋ a tray to put the toys on

What's the maths?

❋ Recognising numerals

❋ Counting

How to play

1. Arrange the hoops in a circle with a number card in each.

2. Put some soft toys in each hoop. There do not have to be the same amount as the hoop number.

3. The children take it in turns to roll the dice, say the number and take one toy from that hoop number.

4. The toy is put on the tray and is now 'out' of the game.

5. The children keep rolling the dice and removing a toy from the hoop of the number shown until one of the hoops is empty.

6. That hoop is the winner. Now, together count how many toys are 'out' on the tray.

Extending the learning
Use number labels 5–10 and a blank dice numbered from 5–10.

Supporting the youngest children's learning
Use three hoops numbered 1–3. The children take turns to pick out a numeral from a bag containing wooden or plastic numerals from 1–3.

Playing the game tomorrow
Extend the game by starting with empty hoops and putting one toy into the hoop with the same number as the dice number rolled. Stop when all the hoops have the right number of toys in.

A game for 2 children

What's the maths?

* ✳ Counting
* ✳ Finding the difference between two numbers
* ✳ Recognising numerals

Beanbag throw

You will need

✳ three beanbags for each player

✳ three large buckets numbered 1, 2, 3

How to play

1. Resource an area with beanbags and large plastic buckets numbered 1, 2, 3.

2. Ask the children to take it in turns to throw the beanbags into the buckets.

3. Talk about and count how many beanbags there are in each bucket and how many thrown beanbags missed a bucket.

Extending the learning
Record on a chalkboard how many beanbags were thrown into each bucket altogether.

Supporting the youngest children's learning
Together, choose one bucket and discuss together what number is on the bucket. Then choose a position close to the bucket to throw from.

Playing the game tomorrow
Collect a numeral or number card every time a beanbag lands in a bucket.

Hunt the welly

You will need

✳ a wellington boot or other object to hide

How to play

1. Set up the game in a part of the outdoor area that has lots of places where things can be hidden.

2. Show the children the object that is going to be hidden – for example, a welly.

3 Ask them to turn round or close their eyes while you hide the welly.

4. While the children are looking for the welly, tell them when they are 'close' or 'far' from finding it. Children take it in turns to be the hider and the finder.

What's the maths?

✳ Using positional words such as 'near', 'far', 'behind', 'under', 'on top of'

Extending the learning
Ask the finder to describe to everyone where they found the welly.

Supporting the youngest children's learning
Be a partner with the children and make suggestions about where to look, such as "I wonder if the welly is hidden under the mat..." and encourage the children to look.

Playing the game tomorrow
This time, hide a teddy and take photographs of where the teddy was found. Make the photographs into a book or a display called 'Looking for Teddy'. The children could use sticky notes to make flaps over the teddy photos.

A game for 2 children

What's the maths?

※ Counting up to six movements

※ Counting up to ten objects

Grid hop

You will need

☀ a 5 × 5 grid chalked onto a hard surface

☀ a collection of small objects such as shells or pebbles

☀ a carrying bag for each hopper

☀ a large 1–6 dice

☀ a person to roll the dice and call out the number

How to play

1. Arrange some objects on each of the squares.

2. Both hoppers stand on a different square.

3. The caller rolls the dice and calls out the number.

4. The hoppers hop that many squares in any direction. If the square they finish their hops on has an object on it, they can pick it up and put it in their bag.

5. When the dice has been rolled five times, the game is over and the hoppers empty their bags and compare their collections.

Extending the learning
Record how many objects each hopper collected.

Supporting the youngest children's learning
Pair the children with a more experienced action counter.

Playing the game tomorrow
Suggest the children select some small-world characters and ask them to arrange them on the grid before the game starts.

High towers

What's the maths?

* ✳ Counting up to 10
* ✳ Measuring height by comparison
* ✳ Recognising numerals

You will need

* ✳ a selection of large bricks
* ✳ a pack of 1–10 cards
* ✳ ten small objects to act as pretend prizes

How to play

1. Shuffle the cards. Each child takes a card and says the number. They then choose and count out that many bricks.

2. Ask the children to each build a tower with their bricks and compare to see which one is the tallest. The tallest tower builder collects a 'prize'.

3. The towers are then demolished.

4. Carry on taking cards, counting out bricks, building towers, comparing and demolishing until all the 'prizes' have been won.

Extending the learning
Provide a metre stick or ruler and a felt-tip pen to mark the height of each tower.

Supporting the youngest children's learning
Ask children to build a tower that is taller than an identified book. Stand the book next to the tower to see if is taller. Tower builders collect a 'prize' if it is taller than the book.

Playing the game tomorrow
Use a 'taller'/'shorter' spinner to decide who is a prizewinner.

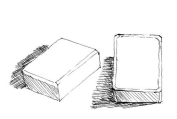

A game for 2 children

Handbags

You will need

※ a large, unnumbered track with twenty squares

※ a collection of handbags positioned along the track. Some squares have more than one handbag.

※ a large 1–6 dice

How to play

1. The children take it in turns to roll the dice and say the number. They then jump that number of squares along the track. If there is a bag on the square when a child finishes jumping, he or she picks it up.

2. The children continue taking turns until both have finished jumping along the track.

3. Ask the children to count how many bags each person has collected.

Extending the learning
Write numerals on the track squares.

Supporting the youngest children's learning
Reduce the track to ten squares and position at least two bags on each square. Use a 1–3 dice.

Playing the game tomorrow
Start the game with six handbags each and put down a bag on every square on the track that you land on. When both children have jumped along the track, count how many squares are without bags.

Sitting on a log

You will need

* six small logs arranged in a circle

* a large 1–6 dice

* 1–5 wooden numerals or number cards

What's the maths?

* Recognising numbers up to 6

How to play

1. Give each child a numeral, then ask them to choose a log to sit on. Sit down on a log with the children. There should be one empty log.

2. Roll the dice, say the number and the child holding that numeral runs and sits on the empty log. If a 6 is rolled, everyone changes logs. Keep playing until everyone is sitting on a different log to the one they started the game on.

Extending the learning

Using the numbers 5–10, turn over number cards and call out the number. Everyone changes logs if a 10 card is called.

Supporting the youngest children's learning

Put a number card on each log and the same numerals in a bag. Children choose a numeral and sit on the log with that number.

Playing the game tomorrow

Roll the dice twice and the two children holding those numbers change logs. If a 6 is one of the numbers rolled, the paired number sits on the empty log.

A game for 2-10 children

What's the maths?

❋ Counting numbers up to ten

❋ Using time words such as 'fast' and 'slow'

Fill the bucket

You will need

❋ a large bucket or plastic container

❋ a collection of beanbags

❋ a washing line

❋ a whistle blower and a one-minute sand timer (optional)

How to play

1. Arrange the washing line in a large circle on the ground and put the bucket in the centre of the circle.

2. Distribute the beanbags singly inside the circle.

3. Ask the children to stand round the edge of the circle.

4. When the whistle blows, the children have to pick up a beanbag and go and put it in the bucket. The whistle blower stands by the bucket and tosses the beanbags out of the bucket one at a time. The children must keep collecting beanbags and putting them in the bucket until the whistle is blown at the end of a minute.

5. If there are more beanbags in the bucket than in the circle, the children are the winners. If there are more beanbags in the circle, the whistle blower is the winner.

Extending the learning
Challenge the children to work out the difference between the number of beanbags in the bucket and in the circle.

Supporting the youngest children's learning
At the end of the game, lay the beanbags in a line and count together.

Playing the game tomorrow
Use between ten and twenty beanbags and time how long it takes to collect all of the beanbags in the bucket. No beanbags are thrown out in this game.

Double dice

A game for 4 children

What's the maths?

* ❋ Recognising numbers
* ❋ Counting and comparing collections

You will need

* ❋ a collection of bricks, plastic small-world figures and counters in six different colours

* ❋ six flags the same colours as the collection objects

* ❋ a colour dice marked in the collection colours

* ❋ a 1–6 dice

How to play

1. The children take it in turns to roll both dice and pick up the number of coloured objects indicated by the dice.

2. Invite the children to line up the objects next to the flag of the same colour.

3. Each child has three goes in turn. Then together count each collection and decide which colour is the winner.

Extending the learning

Challenge the children to put the colour collections in winning order, so that the colour with the most objects wins, the next highest number comes second, and so on.

Supporting the youngest children's learning

The children have three turns each and make individual collections, deciding which colour has most in each collection.

Playing the game tomorrow

Use different objects and different colours.

details. Encourage the children to describe the locations of things such as a very tall tree or the best place to touch lots of circles or make an interesting pattern-rubbing.

Where's the learning in maths trails?

Maths trails give children an opportunity to look at things from a different viewpoint. The scope is endless, and trails can be made to suit a particular topic or group of children. Trails encourage children as they begin to collaborate and work in a group as, they modify and make a maths trail accessible to all children.

You can make a maths trail to suit any part of your maths curriculum, whether it's searching for shapes that have been previously hidden on site or walking along the street looking for numbers or taking photos of squares. Routes, walks and pathways have an obvious link to maths, especially when we use words such as 'straight on', 'turn', 'reverse' to describe the walk or the route. Walking together on a route where the emphasis is on looking for the maths will extend children's observational skills and their mathematical thinking and vocabulary.

Suggestions for maths trails

Colour trail: For the younger children, put together a colour trail and provide colour charts to support the discussion. As you walk around the outdoor area, discuss the colours of the things you pass. You could link this to a colour street walk where a walk record is produced and the children identify and colour in different front doors. Use the opportunity to count how many red doors or blue doors they see.

Photographic trail: Make a photographic trail. This can be a series of photographs displayed on a fence with a notice saying 'If you see one of the following, come and describe where you saw it'. Alternatively, the photographs can be made into a booklet for children to explore the designated area using the booklet as an 'I-Spy' book.

Arrow trail: Use twigs to make an arrow trail and ask children to report back on where the trail went and encourage them to make their own trail. Paint arrows on large stones or pebbles collected from the beach and lay a trail around the setting grounds. The following week, invite the children to rearrange the stones to make a different route. Discuss with the children the difference between the two routes.

Footprint path: Make a footprint path to encourage children to explore all parts of the outdoor environment. Fix the footprints to asphalt using Bluetak or cut them from heavy card to use on grass or earth. Discuss with the children which route they took. For younger children, make colour footprints to follow and ask them to report back on what they found at the end of the path.

Number trail: Make a numeral path for younger children to follow. Choose a number and make a trail using several of the same wooden or plastic numerals. Invite the children to make their own one-number trail using either paper numerals or, for a more permanent trail, wooden numerals or numbers painted on the ground.

For older children, the trail can be made from numeral cards that the children have to follow in order. Make the trail last longer by hiding the cards at different heights. You could make a numeral trail on a grass area by writing the numbers on plastic seed cards and pushing them into the ground.

Go on a number hunt — look for numbers in order or search for the same number. Record by drawing, rubbing or photographing where the numbers were seen. Older children could take clipboards, pencils and paper with them and write down the numbers they see.

Wheel walk: Go for a wheel walk and look for wheels in the local environment. Talk about circles, cylinders, small- and large-sized wheels. Decide on how many wheels most cars have and how many wheels lorries, buses and cycles have.

Pattern walk: Take photographs of different patterns that the children can find and then put them together in a zigzag book, explaining where other children can see them outdoors. Provide pieces of patterned metal or wood that can be fixed to the wall and leaves and twigs for children to use in their own patterns. When the wall is complete, ask children to explore the patterns with their fingers and explain what the pattern feels like.

Scavenger walk: Go with the children on a scavenger hunt. Display the collections that were found and identify where the items were found. Children could do this either by drawing their own treasure maps or by putting a cross on a communal map.

Obstacle course: Construct an obstacle course with the children. Use obstacles to walk through, across, under and on. Involve any climbing-frame equipment as part of the obstacle course and discuss ways of crawling over, under and through.

Luminous trail: Use luminous paint and make spots to mark out a trail. Use torches to follow the spots.

Wool trail: Make a trail to follow by tying thick wool at children's waist height and winding round trees, posts and drainpipes. Try to zigzag the trail across the area. Invite the children to follow the trail by holding the wool in their hands.

River-bed trail: Construct a riverbed trail. Lay a narrow trail of pebbles, gravel and small stones across a tarmac area and ask children to walk the length of the riverbed and describe what it feels like.

Chapter 5

Problem solving in the outdoor environment

Encouraging investigation

In order to develop thinking skills, problem solving needs to be built into our everyday provision, not just added on as an extra. You will want the children to investigate the environment in small ways. You can start by using everyday experiences to support children's counting or by discussing with them the best way to pick up leaves or in which direction to turn the tap to increase water flow. The

children will be able to connect their mathematical ideas and understanding while finding out about the environment by making patterns, comparing, categorising and classifying. You will help them to become mathematically creative not just by setting challenges but by allowing children to set challenges for themselves.

The role of collaboration

Children need lots of opportunities to investigate maths ideas and the situations in which to apply them. They will find this more beneficial if they are encouraged to work collaboratively to solve problems. Discuss with the children how to tackle a particular problem and how to work as a team or a pair. In this way, children have some input and control over their own learning as well as having the freedom to explore mathematical ideas through play.

Extending the learning

Our role as adults is crucial in sustaining children's interest and challenging their ideas. You can extend children's thinking by raising new questions and helping them to evaluate their findings. It will be particularly helpful if, when the children are engaged in the activity, you model the key vocabulary using descriptive and comparative language. Ask open-ended questions about how things work and why they are happening.

> **Ten helpful questions to ask when children are problem solving**
>
> ❋ What will you need?
> ❋ Can you tell us about...?
> ❋ What was the first thing you did?
> ❋ Can you say anything you noticed about...?
> ❋ I wonder what will happen next...?
> ❋ Can you guess what...?
> ❋ Can you explain...?
> ❋ What can we say about...?
> ❋ What would you see if...?
> ❋ What could we try next?

Explaining, talking and discussing are a very important part of learning maths and a valuable life skill. We should focus on creating situations that support discussion and be sure to ask open-ended questions such as "I wonder what will happen when...?" We need to encourage children to use descriptive language, and you can extend children's conversations by encouraging them to say what they are doing and why. All young children need to talk about and reflect on their experiences.

Autonomous problem solving

So that your children can get the greatest benefit and become adept problem solvers when they are working in the outdoor area, they should be able to access the resources autonomously and independently. Encourage children to carry out their own risk assessments. Reflect the information back to the children so that they can clarify together and decide on possible solutions. Provide materials that encourage children to involve themselves without adult intervention, such as an old camera or a real telephone.

Problem solving is an integral part of early years experiences. Children identify a problem, make a plan, implement it and then evaluate its effectiveness. To do this, children need experience with a wide range of materials using a multi-sensory approach. Taking photographs provides an opportunity for children to recall the experience.

A diversity of materials can ensure that children with different needs have adequate provision. For children learning English as an additional language, imaginative play and problem-solving scenarios will provide rich mathematical experiences.

Assessing children's problem solving and investigations

The initial stages of problem solving
Do the children show signs of knowing what the problem is about? The first step in solving any problem is an understanding of what the problem is — this is also a crucial stage in the solution process.

A useful technique for helping children understand the problem is to ask them or their learning partner to say what the problem is in their own words or to describe something about it.

With more experience, the initial stage of problem solving generally involves doodling, sketching, estimating, measuring, counting, asking questions, talking, listening and looking. You will see some children engaged in some of these activities as they become involved in the problem.

Having a plan

You will also be observing whether the children show signs of having a plan. Once the problem situation has been untangled and identified, the children will hopefully be offering ways of solving, and this might need careful scaffolding. The trial-and-error method is widely used by people of all ages and can be quite efficient for certain types of problems. Its most obvious advantage is its simplicity which makes it well suited for use by young children.

Mathematical skills and knowledge

You will want to identify what mathematical knowledge and skills the children used, whether they were being systematic and organised within the limits of their maturity and whether they used any tools as support.

The practitioner's role

* Help children accept the challenge of problem solving — a problem is not a problem until you want to solve it.

* Build a supportive atmosphere — children need to tackle the unfamiliar without feeling threatened when they become stuck.

* Provide a framework within which children can reflect.

* Make sure that every child feels successful – children learn more effectively when they discuss and think about their experiences.

Making a record

Children need a way of representing the problem either concretely, pictorially or verbally so that these images can be recalled, revisited, remembered and built on when solving future problems.

Learning with children

You do not need to be an expert problem solver to support children in acquiring problem-solving skills. The primary role of early years specialists is to establish a non-threatening environment. You must also have the courage to learn along with the children and be open to divergent thinking and alternative ways of solving things.

Solving real problems

Using number, data and measurement skills
when sorting out the clothes

"How can we sort out the outdoor clothing box?"

"How can we pair up the wellington boots?"

"Estimate how many hats and gloves we need."

"Investigate which clothes are suitable for outdoor play on wet days."

"Use a hand lens to look closely at both sides of rainproof fabrics. Feel the texture and discuss whether it is rough or smooth."

"Try to make or find a patchwork hat or cloak to wear outdoors on rainy days."

Using measurement, counting and data
to investigate snails

"How can we find out what snails eat?"

"Put some snails on some damp plastic sheeting and measure how fast a snail moves. Estimate how many snails we can find in five minutes."

Additionally, you will want to resource any role-play area with writing materials so that children can make lists of phone numbers. Children will also need calculators to encourage discussion about numbers and costs, as well as money to go shopping with at any outdoor market stall that is set up. Food stalls and ice-cream vendors need takeaway menus as well as price lists and order slips.

You will want to plan opportunities for the children to listen to stories that contain mathematical elements such as *Mr Gumpy's Outing*. The children should then be able to retell the story independently, using story props to develop the narrative and make decisions such as what the characters do next or how the story might end. A story bag doesn't have to be based around a book — it could be a collection of objects linked to the same topic or theme such as an autumn box or a dinosaur resource box.

Art outdoors

An outdoor art workshop needs to be an area full of exciting and imaginative materials. It should be a place where aspiring artists can explore, experiment and build up a range of art skills and experiences while learning some maths. Provide resources that allow play activities to evolve. For example, the next activity takes advantage of children's interest in puddles.

Sweep up paint

You will need

* a concrete or hard surface

* a large shallow tray and duct tape (optional)

* water and paint

* sticks to mix the paint

* a variety of brooms and paint rollers

What to do

1. Create a puddle on the hard surface by either filling a shallow indentation in the surface with water or by attaching a large shallow tray to the surface with duct tape and filling it with water.

2. Introduce paint into the 'puddle' and use sticks to mix the paint and water, making sure it is a runny consistency (otherwise, it will take time when you want to remove the paint from the concrete).

3. Provide the children with large foam decorating rollers, small hand brooms and yard brooms to paint swirls and lines over the concrete.

The question to ask and the problem to solve

Is it possible make a zigzag line when you are using a roller?

Highlighted vocabulary:

straight lines, curved lines, spirals, colour names, rough, smooth,

Key learning intentions

* Solving problems involving shape and space

* Exploring colour, texture and shape

Enhancing the water area

Pebbles and small stones are smooth and satisfying to touch and handle. They also darken in colour when they are wet. Encourage children to slide pebbles individually into the water tank and make observations of the changes in the pebbles. Ask questions such as 'Does it run faster down a steeper slope?'

Highlighted vocabulary:

more, less, full, empty, close, near, far, pour, share, together, agree

Key learning intentions

* Solving problems involving time and data
* Working systematically

Water divining

You will need

* two large water containers — one containing water

* a selection of jugs, sponges, long lengths of plastic guttering, empty plastic pop bottles and plastic tubing

* watering cans

* measuring sticks, ribbons and tapes

What to do

1. Position two water trays a small distance apart (less than the length of the guttering). One of the trays should be full up with water and the other nearly empty.

2. Ask the children to transfer the water from one container to the other.

The question to ask and the problem to solve
How far apart are the two containers?
What's your idea for transferring the water?

Ice blocks

You will need

* four small-world characters such as plastic dinosaurs that have been frozen in an ice-cube tray.

* four small containers

* oven gloves, tongs, scoops

* pencils and paper for possible recording

* sand-timers, stopwatches, clocks, tockers

What to do

1. Put one frozen dinosaur in each container and put each container in a different place such as in the shade, in the sun, underneath a blanket and indoors.

2. Discuss with the children what dinosaur cube will melt first.

The question to ask and the problem to solve

How can we remember in what order the dinosaur cubes melted?

Which cube took the shortest time and which dinosaur the longest time?

Highlighted vocabulary:

long time, short time, melt, more, less, inside, outside, hot, cold, warm, sun, light, dark

Key learning intentions

* Solving problems involving time and data

* Asking questions about why things happen and how things work

Ten ideas to enrich the mathematics in water play

Enrichment	Mathematics	Questions to ask
Introduce plastic numerals and sieves.	Using some number names in play	*Do you think you've sieved any numbers that are the same?*
Throw in handfuls of plastic coins and sieve them out again.	Beginning to count up how many coins altogether	*How can you find out how much money you've caught?*
Make holes in the sides of a plastic bottle and watch how the water spurts out of them.	Commenting on and compare the lengths of two water spurts	*I wonder which of the water spurts is the longest...*
Sometimes use small plastic washing-up bowls. Resource with eye droppers and toy tea sets.	Using words such as 'full', 'half full' and 'empty' to discuss while filling and emptying containers	*How will you know when the cup is full?*
Add bubbles, spoons and containers. Try to capture the bubbles on the spoons.	Talking about weight using appropriate words and discussing which container holds the most bubbles	*I wonder how we could find out how much the bubbles weigh?*
In summer, stir a bag of ice cubes into the water.	Talking about time and measuring time	*Do you think the ice will be melted by lunchtime?*
Float different-sized plastic lids with a punched hole and see how long they take to sink.	Talking about shape and size	*What surprised you when the lids were in the water?*
Use coloured plastic balls and balloon pumps and have ball races.	Using 'first', 'second', 'last' to describe position in race	*How can we remember which order the balls came in the race?*
Connect real plastic pipes together and stand in a tray.	Discussing routes the water will take through the pipes	*How can we work out which pipe the water will come from?*
Add various plastic and rubber gloves and jugs.	Experimenting with filling and emptying different-sized gloves	*Is there a way of deciding which glove holds the most water?*

Enhancing the sand area

Sand is endlessly fascinating, especially in the way it changes its behaviour, depending on how much water is added.

When dry sand is stirred or poured, it flows rather like a liquid and gradually finds a level, whereas pouring damp sand is a non-starter — it just falls in irregular lumps. Children need to have access to both types of sand when they are playing outdoors.

Set up your own seaside in the summer and use it for counting and estimating as well as having fun.

Sand patterns

You will need

* one shallow tray of dry sand
* one shallow tray of damp sand
* a collection of plastic combs and rakes
* two or three balloon pumps

What to do

1. Make designs in either or both trays of sand using the combs and rakes.
2. Use a balloon pump to blow across the surface of the trays and talk about what happens.

The question to ask and the problem to solve
Can you make wavy patterns in both trays?

What happened to the sand when you blew across it? Is it the same effect in both trays?

Highlighted vocabulary:

pattern, round, straight, curved, over, under, through, across, same, different

Key learning intentions

* Talking about simple patterns
* Looking closely at similarities, patterns and change

Highlighted vocabulary:

guess how many, nearly, about the same as, estimate, wet, dry, damp, smooth, rough

Key learning intentions

❋ Estimating a number in range that can be counted reliably

❋ Checking by counting

❋ Investigating objects and material by using all of their senses

On the beach

You will need

❋ a shallow, rigid pond liner

❋ one large piece of flexible pond liner

❋ a large quantity of slightly damp sand

❋ one bag of mixed pebbles and shells

❋ imitation railway sleepers

What to do

1. Use a flexible pond liner as a base for some sand and four railway sleepers to surround the sand to stop it encroaching on the whole area.

2. Place the rigid pond liner in the middle of the flexible pond liner and fill with water to make a sea, complete with some large shells and pebbles.

3. Scatter items on the beach to be 'found'. Beachcombers will need to remove their socks and shoes.

4. As an extra, a large umbrella and ice-cream seller's table will provide lots of opportunities for calculating the cost of cornets, ice lollies and drinks.

The question to ask and the problem to solve
How can we find out how many footprints you made from the water to the ice-cream stall? How many do you guess it will be?

Ten ideas to enrich the mathematics in sand play

Enrichment	Mathematics	Questions to ask
Bury treasure such as charity shop jewellery. Wear pirate hats to dig up the treasure and weigh how much was found.	Talking about weight and using words such as heavy and light.	*I wonder what we can use to weigh the jewellery you dug up…*
Colour-streak the sand by mixing dry sand, powder paint and water together.	Filling and emptying small cups of sand. Using words 'full' and 'empty'.	*How will you know when the cup is full up?*
Use individual sand trays with small world characters to make families.	Using the vocabulary involved in adding and subtracting.	*How many people altogether are you going to put in your sand tray?*
Bury metal items and provide magnets as metal detectors.	Identifying the properties of a collection.	*Could you tell me if any of the things that you found are the same?*
Introduce large sequins and small stones so that the sand has a gritty texture. Provide different-sized containers to fill.	Using words such as 'heavier' and 'lighter' to compare quantities.	*I wonder which of your boxes is the heaviest?*
Make lots of different-sized sand pies on a shallow builders tray and provide an assortment of cutting implements for slicing the pies.	Solving problems using halving and doubling.	*How many pieces did you have when you cut your pie in half?*
Resource the sand area with a variety of spades, containers, flags on sticks and windmills.	Beginning to estimate using the language of size.	*How big do you think your sand castle will be?*
Resource dry sand with a wide variety of different-sized boots and shoes (such as ballet shoes and wellington boots) to fill up and empty out.	Using words such as 'full', 'half full' and 'empty'.	*Is your boot more than half full?*
Resource a container of dry silver sand with a variety of different-sized sieves.	Using words related to time such as 'quickly' and 'slowly'.	*Did you notice if any of the sieves emptied the sand really slowly?*
Station a pulley system and climbing frame next to the sand area.	Using words related to length and height such 'high' and 'low' and 'near' and 'far'.	*Which bucket did you think felt the heaviest?*

Enhancing the garden or wildlife area

The garden area provides real opportunities for maths activities with a special focus on measuring skills. As children become involved in planting and noting plant growth, they also become involved in ecological and conservation issues and notice seasonal changes. Support the children's care for living things by sharing their joy in discovering mini-beasts in their natural habitats. Draw their attention to natural occurrences such as how trees and leaves change in the autumn. Spend some time in autumn collecting falling leaves. Pick up handfuls of leaves and scrunch them up. Listen to the sound the dry leaves make as they rustle and discuss the difference in the look and size of a whole leaf and a scrunched one.

Highlighted vocabulary:

count, how many?,
one more, one less,
float, drift, fall, drop

Key learning intentions

* Beginning to count beyond 10
* Saying a number that is one more or one less than a given number
* Finding out about events they observe

Dry leaves

You will need

* access to a heap of leaves
* a small plastic bucket

What to do

1. Fill a small bucket with fallen leaves.

2. Stand on a climbing frame or a bench and empty the bucketful of dry leaves into the air. See how many can be caught before they fall on the ground.

The question to ask and a problem to solve
How many leaves did you catch? How many leaves would you have if I gave you one more? I wonder if there are more leaves that were caught or more leaves fallen on the ground...

Keeping woodlice

You will need

※ a collecting container such as a plastic ice-cream tub

※ a plastic fish tank or other transparent container

※ a plastic spoon

※ plastic sandwich wrap

※ damp earth, stones, leaves, twigs and moss

※ food for woodlice, such as apples or carrots

※ plant water-spray

※ clipboard and paper for recording

※ woodlice (found under stones, dead leaves or pieces of wood)

What to do

1. First, set up your woodlice home by arranging the earth, leaves, twigs and moss across the bottom of the fish tank. Try to replicate the place where they will be found.

2. Go on a woodlice hunt — search round the base of trees, under old wood, stones, bricks or damp leaves. Pick up the woodlice with a plastic spoon (not fingers, or they may be harmed) and put them in the collecting box.

3. Collect about ten woodlice and put them in the tank as quickly as possible.

4. Cover the top of the tank with cling film and make sure there are air holes in the cling film.

5. Count how many woodlice are put in the tank.

6. Once a day, spray the earth in the tank lightly with water.

7. Every day, count and record how many woodlice can be seen in the tank. Discuss how many are moving about, how many are curled up and how many are hidden.

The question to ask and the problem to solve
How many woodlice can you see altogether? How can we find out how many woodlice are hidden?

Highlighted vocabulary:

altogether, how many?, the difference between, add, take away, living, looking, listening, crawl, roll

Key learning intentions

※ Using language related to addition and subtraction

※ Using addition and subtraction to find totals

※ Finding out about some features of living things

※ Using talk to clarify thinking and ideas

Highlighted vocabulary:

wormery, earth,
full, empty,
about the same as,
too much, too little,
observations, sightings,
next to, behind, front,
back, under

Key learning intentions

* ❋ Use size language
* ❋ Use everyday words to describe position
* ❋ Find out about some features of living things
* ❋ Extend their vocabulary, exploring the meanings and sounds of new words

A wormery

You will need

❋ six tall waterproof containers such as empty one-litre plastic drink bottles with the tops cut off or plastic sweet jars

❋ a black plastic bag or bin liner and six elastic bands to make covers for the top of the containers

❋ commercial compost mixture (such as John Innes No 3) or enough earth to fill each container three-quarters full

❋ 1–6 number labels

❋ clipboards and paper

What to do

1. To make a pleasant home for worms, the children will need to partly fill the containers with earth or compost mixture and look for two or three worms to put in the bucket.

2. Use the black plastic to make covers for the tops of the containers. Don't forget to make air holes in each top.

3. Put a number label next to each container.

4. Water the earth sparingly every day with fresh water and put leaves and grass cuttings on the top.

5. Make regular observations of worm sightings and record the container number and position of each sighting.

Ten ideas to enrich the mathematics in the garden area

Enrichment	Mathematics	Questions to ask
Keep goldfish in a large container.	Counting a random collection.	*How many goldfish can you see?*
Introduce a bird tray.	Collecting information and data.	*How will you remember which birds came to the bird table?*
Resource the area with at least two wheelbarrows.	Using everyday words such as 'next to' to describe position.	*Can you explain where you collected your wheelbarrow load from?*
Dig a shallow pond to encourage wildlife.	Collecting information and data.	*Have you seen more ladybirds than ants today?*
Plant food plants such as tomatoes and runner beans in grow bags.	Explaining how to measure using sticks and tapes.	*I wonder how we can find out if the tallest plant has the most tomatoes growing on it...*
Plant fast-growing plants of different heights, such as sunflowers.	Using words such as 'taller' and 'shorter' when comparing and ordering heights.	*Can you suggest what we could use to measure the height of the plants?*
Position small figures such as gnomes or toadstools.	Using position words such as 'close', 'far apart', 'near'.	*Can you explain where you have put the gnomes?*
Make a pathway using individual stepping stones.	Counting and using words related to addition and subtraction such as 'altogether'.	*How can we find out how many stepping stones you have put down and how many are left?*
Provide a potting table resourced with different-sized pots.	Using words such as 'biggest', 'smallest' and 'middle-sized' to compare sizes.	*Which sized pot are you going to use for your bulb?*
Provide trugs and baskets to collect grasses, acorns, flower heads and leaves.	In discussion, begin to use the vocabulary involved in adding and subtracting, and comparison.	*How many flowers have you got altogether?*

Spectaculars

One way of creating excitement in the outdoor area is by planning a 'spectacular'. This could be an exciting one-off or temporary event, an exhibition or a permanent exhibit: invite an artist or potter to visit; set up an ice or sand sculpture, an engine or other machine, a growing willow house or chair, or a giant piñata. Involving children in 'spectaculars' heightens the excitement, and an activity such as setting off rocket balloons together certainly achieves this. This is a very easy spectacle to set up and it generates lots of mathematical and scientific discussion as well as being, well, spectacular.

Highlighted vocabulary:

fast, slow, stop, go, further, straight line, quicker, before, after, air, pump, full, empty, inflate, release

Key learning intentions

※ Talk about time and speed

※ Respond to significant experiences

※ Ask questions about why things work

Fast rocket balloons

You will need

※ 1 metre of thin string (let the children measure this)

※ one wide, plastic straw

※ masking tape

※ one long balloon and a balloon pump

※ one plastic peg

※ two support posts (a tree and a climbing frame will do)

What to do

1. Thread the string through the straw.

2. Tie each end of the string to a support post so that the string is taut.

3. Blow up the balloon and put the peg on the end (to stop the air escaping).

4. Tape the balloon to the straw.

5. Move the straw to one end of the string.

6. Take the peg off the end of the balloon and watch how fast the balloon hurtles along the string.

Chapter 7

Observing and resourcing children's play outdoors

Observing outdoor learning

Mathematical play in the foundation stage is enhanced by an outdoor environment where maths is integrated with the other areas of learning. Using the outdoor area gives children a chance to acquire first-hand sensory knowledge of the natural world. There are opportunities to engage in really messy play and physically, they can climb, jump and swing while imaginative and creative play all provide a backdrop for experiencing and understanding mathematics.

Promoting mathematical development and drawing out the mathematical learning in a range of activities that initially support other areas of learning will be easier if the mathematical potential has been already identified. Observing and enhancing the mathematical learning, the activities and the challenges in the outdoor environment will be part of the responsibility of the team who are working with the children. Your observations will reflect the child -initiated play that develops from what has been planned for the outdoor area and also the play that develops from children's interests.

> **Mathematical aspects of some patterns of behaviour you can observe in children's play**
>
> ✳ Transporting (carrying things from one place to another using a truck, dolls pram, pushchair or bag)
>
> ✳ Positioning (placing objects carefully)
>
> ✳ Orientation (turning and placing objects)
>
> ✳ Horizontality, verticality, diagonality, circularity (in building, drawing or mark-making)
>
> ✳ Enclosure (making enclosures with bricks, blocks, crates)
>
> ✳ Enveloping or wrapping
>
> ✳ Rotation (turning keys, knobs, wheels, taps)
>
> ✳ Connections (joining things together)

Observational assessment

Exploring maths as part of the outdoor curriculum gives you the opportunity to develop children's personal, social and emotional well-being as well as promoting positive attitudes and enthusiasm for mathematical understanding. You will be able to observe children working together harmoniously as part of a team or small group as well as encouraging them to listen and talk to each other in a wide variety of outdoor situations.

In promoting children's activity-based learning, you will be providing activities that are both challenging and achievable. You will be able to observe and monitor children's mathematical understanding as well as respond to children's personal, social and emotional development.

It is essential to have in mind the kind of mathematical developments that are likely to occur in the different outdoor areas. You will want to identify other areas of development as well, such as PSE. Examples of what to look for in sample areas are in the following table. You may just observe quietly, but often you'll need to engage the children in conversation to find out about their thinking.

Examples of observation to be made in outdoor areas

Child-initiated play in sand area

PSE	Maths	Questions to ask
Show curiosity... Tackle self-chosen challenges.	Use positional and size language.	*I wonder how many spoonfuls it will take to fill up the box...*
Manage appropriate tasks.	Offer comments and ask questions.	*How are we going to find out which mug holds the most?*
Show high level of involvement.	Use language of measurement.	*Perhaps we could weigh the buckets. What shall we use?*

Building towers using outdoor construction materials

PSE	Maths	Questions to ask
Show willingness to tackle problems.	Use positional and size language.	*What are you going to use to build your tower?*
Show independence selecting and carrying out activities.	Use shapes appropriately.	*What would happen if you balanced a cone on your tower?*
Persist for extended periods of time.	Order items by height.	*How can you be sure that your tower is the taller than the chair?*

Playing with a hand puppet

PSE	Maths	Questions to ask
Share experiences. Show curiosity.	Shows interest in numbers and counting.	*Puppet asks children if they have ever counted anything.*
Take initiative.	Uses some number names.	*Puppet asks children to help him count.*
Initiate interactions with other people.	Spot errors in counting and number order.	*Puppet asks children if his counting is good.*

Resources to enhance the maths play

As well as choosing resources that are appropriate for a diverse range of abilities, you will need to consider your provision for children with special educational needs. You will also need to consider the support that is offered, such as additional space, access or adult time.

The following table lists resources that will promote enriched play and mathematical learning.

Maths resource suggestions

Number	
• Skittles, quoits, beanbags, traffic cones • Range of small balls in assorted colours, large balls, goal nets, large buckets • Collections of natural objects such as pebbles, pine cones, shells • Seeds, bulbs, plant pots and compost • Sticky cards for collecting small natural objects, bug boxes and magnifiers • Small-world characters such as dinosaurs, toy cars, animals • Washing line and pegs to suspend clothes, plastic bottles, tin cans, small plastic buckets • Picnic sets • Number games • Large dice, large spinners, large numbered carpet tiles • Number tiles, wooden and plastic numerals • Laminated number lines • Large board games and floor games • Conkers, acorns, sycamore seeds, shells and leaves • 1–100 number square • Large dominoes • Wall games (such as Ludo, Noughts and crosses, Four in a line, Snakes and Ladders) with magnetic counters	• Large bucket balances • Equipment in a range of sizes (spades, spoons, scoops, tongs) • Nesting cups, funnels, cardboard tubes, colanders and sieves • Watering cans, hose, squeezy bottles, plastic bottles, gutters and tubing • Ribbons, tapes, measuring sticks, surveyor's tapes **Shape and space** • Large wooden building blocks, large stacking plastic bricks • Large cardboard boxes • Crates, planks and barrels • Tyres of varying sizes • Selection of large and small 2D and 3D shapes, including shapes to sit on • Small wooden logs (as sold for fires) **Recording and data collection** • Clipboards, paper, pens and pencils • Easels • Pavement chalks • Brushes and cans for water • Hanging baskets with wooden numerals • Small plastic cubes and counters • Empty plastic boxes and buckets • Large squared grid paper and felt-tip pens • Threading balls and beads and interlocking cubes for keeping count
Measures	
• Coloured gravel, sand, wood shavings, bark chippings • Washing-up bowls and buckets	